The Philosophy of
Tai Chi Chuan

The
PHILOSOPHY
of
Tai Chi Chuan

Wisdom from Confucius, Lao Tzu,
& Other Great Thinkers

Freya and Martin Boedicker

Blue Snake Books
Berkeley, California

Published by Blue Snake Books
an imprint of North Atlantic Books
Berkeley, California

Cover and book design by Susan Quasha
Cover calligraphy by Huang Zhongjun
Printed in the United States of America

The Philosophy of Tai Chi Chuan: Wisdom from Confucius, Lao Tzu, and Other Great Thinkers is sponsored and published by the Society for the Study of Native Arts and Sciences (dba North Atlantic Books), an educational non-profit based in Berkeley, California, that collaborates with partners to develop cross-cultural perspectives, nurture holistic views of art, science, the humanities, and healing, and seed personal and global transformation by publishing work on the relationship of body, spirit, and nature.

North Atlantic Books' publications are available through most bookstores. For further information, call 800-733-3000 or visit our website at www.northatlanticbooks.com. or www.bluesnakebooks.com.

Library of Congress Cataloging-in-Publication Data
　　Boedicker, Freya, 1970–
　　[Philosophisches lesebuch zum Tai chi chuan. English]
　　The philosophy of Tai chi chuan : wisdom from Confucius, Lao Tzu, and other great thinkers / Freya and Martin Boedicker.
　　　　p. cm.
　　ISBN 978-1-58394-263-5
　　1. Philosophy, Chinese—To 221 B.C. 2. Tai chi. I. Boedicker, Martin, 1965– II. Title. III. Title: Wisdom from Confucius, Lao Tzu, and other great thinkers.
　　B126.B55 2009
　　181'.11—dc22　　　　　　　　　　　　　　　　　　2008038862

3 4 5 6 7 8 9 SHERIDAN 22 21 20 19 18

Acknowledgments

The greatest thanks to our teachers:
Ma Jiangbao
(Wu Tai Chi Chuan)

Armin Sievers
(East-Asia-Science)

Dr. Yanqian von der Lippe-Fan
(Chinese language)

And to our editor:
Kit Gerould

This book would not exist without them.

Contents

Introduction

Introduction

TAI CHI CHUAN, THE ART AND the practice, is deeply imbued with Chinese philosophy. To learn Tai Chi Chuan is therefore not only to have the adventure of engaging in an exotic form of movement, but also of encountering the profound ideas of Chinese culture and tradition.

It is certainly very fruitful to break away from what is common and taken for granted and to open oneself to new ideas. The rich philosophical thinking of ancient China has fascinated the West for centuries. Those who practice Tai Chi Chuan can experience these ideas in a very special way, because the movements express key concepts of Chinese philosophy. This book should make the close relationship between the philosophical concepts and Tai Chi Chuan even clearer.

We start with a short overview of the history of Chinese philosophy. This is followed by twelve philosophical texts. Each of the twelve is introduced briefly, and then we present parts of the original texts, which have been chosen because they have significance for the student of Tai Chi Chuan.

Throughout this book, we use consistent English translations for Chinese philosophical terms. The Chinese term appears in parentheses following the translation of the concept. These concepts play an important role in Tai Chi Chuan, and they get individual and specific attention in an extensive glossary at the end of the book.

The spelling *Tai Chi Chuan* is now common in the West, and thus we use that spelling consistently in this book. We have avoided the spelling *Taijiquan* or others to avoid confusion. The pinyin transliteration is used for all other Chinese terms.

After studying this book the reader will have a better understanding of the world of ideas of Tai Chi Chuan, providing new inspiration for his or her training.

We hope you enjoy this book. It has been a great pleasure to write it.

FREYA AND MARTIN BOEDICKER

A Brief History
of Chinese Philosophy

ACCORDING TO CHINESE HISTORICAL TRADITION, CHINA is said to have been ruled in the third millennium BC by mythic emperors. These included Emperors Fu Xi, Shen Nong, Huang Di (known as the Yellow Emperor), and Yu the Great, who allegedly founded the Xia Dynasty.

Around 2000 BC the first signs of a highly developed civilization began to emerge. In the middle of this millennium, the Shang Dynasty was in power. For the first time, bronze was produced. From this period, texts of oracles survive, carved on the backs of turtles, bronze containers, and bones.

In the eleventh century BC the Shang Dynasty was overthrown by the Zhou tribe. In the following period, the Zhous introduced feudal rule.

The decline of the Zhou Dynasty in the fifth century BC led to the emergence of a series of smaller states. Because of continuous strife and wars between the feudal lords, the time from approximately 480 BC until the unification of the realm in 221

BC is called the "period of the warring states." It was a time of hunger and turmoil because of the ongoing wars. The invention of iron and of the plough, along with the introduction of monetary economics and consequent changes, fueled efforts to find new ways of living and new values.

The changes in society resulted in manifold forms of intellectual life. This time is also called the "time of the hundred schools of philosophy." At no other time before had speculative thinking been cherished and promoted to such an extent. The competition between different intellectual trends reflects the external conflicts of the time. Among the schools one finds famous representatives such as the Confucians *(rujia)*, the Mohists *(mojia)*, and the Daoists *(daojia)*, as well as the Yin-Yang School *(yinyangjia)*, the Legalists *(fajia)*, the Dialecticans *(mingjia)*, and the Strategists of War *(bingjia)*. Their central themes became social life, the ideal order, and the relationship between human beings and nature. Teaching was based on dialogue, edifying anecdotes, and examples taken from daily life. The plethora of schools of philosophy was not to survive China's political unification in 221 BC.

In 221 BC the state of Qin conquered its last rival. Under its lord, from then on called Qin Shi Huangdi, the first unified Chinese state emerged. During the Qin Dynasty, feudalism was abolished in order to promote the process of unification. Measures, laws, and writing systems were harmonized. The Legalist School based on Han Feizi was made the state philosophy. The Legalist School was not concerned with moral questions; its aim was to establish binding laws for everyone and thus to establish a stable political system unified under one ruler. The other schools of philosophy were persecuted and their books and documents burned. Following the death of its first ruler, Emperor Qin Shi Huangdi, in 210 BC, the dynasty declined and the Han Dynasty was established.

The Han Dynasty (206 BC–220 AD) severed links with the Legalist School. At the beginning of the dynasty, Liu An, the uncle of the first Han emperor, introduced the work of Daoist Huainanzi. However, this was not accepted as the dominant philosophy. A slightly altered form of Confucianism became the new state philosophy.

One of the leaders of this Han-Confucianism, which is also called New-Text School, was Dong Zhongshu. He systematically described the connection of heaven, man, and earth—that is, between nature and social life. He merged in a complicated way the old Confucianism with the ideas of other schools, such as the Yin-Yang School.

In terms of philosophical history, the Han Dynasty is usually categorized as a neo-classical time because its discussions frequently refer to the "old" schools. However, it should be noted that although no completely new school was founded and despite referring back to classical works, traditions were frequently changed drastically.

The end of the Han Dynasty in 220 AD heralded a time of disharmony and schism lasting for almost 400 years. China split into a series of short-lived states and dynasties. The spiritual and moral vacuum of this time was filled by Neo-Daoism and by Buddhism, which came from India. The center of the Neo-Daoists was a movement consisting mainly of artists and philosophers called "The Seven Sages of the Bamboo Grove."

This movement rejected social and civic duties, demonstrating this attitude by deliberately provoking the public. The Sui (581–618 AD) and Tang (618–906 AD) Dynasties ended the time of disharmony. A strong central state supported by a system of examinations for civil servants as a way of recruiting a ruling elite emerged. It was during the Tang Dynasty that Buddhism reached its peak in China.

Following the ninth century AD the adversaries of Buddhism focused on Confucianism again. During the Song Dynasty (960–1279 AD) leading philosophers like Zhou Dunyi, Shao Yong, and Zhu Xi merged the ideas of Buddhism and Daoism with Confucianism. This resulted in the so-called Neo-Confucianism. The articulation and interpretation of this philosophy was based on Zhu Xi and became the new state philosophy.

In the Yuan Dynasty (1280–1368 AD) China was conquered by the Mongols and fell for the first time under foreign rule. Politically these were interesting times, but philosophically speaking there were no new developments. During the Ming Dynasty (1368–1644 AD) Zhu Xi's school of rationalism dominated, but gradually Wang Shouren's idealist Neo-Confucianist School became a leading competitor for influence.

Under the Qing Dynasty (1644–1911 AD) China was conquered by the Manchurians. This was the peak of China's economic and political development. Confucianism remained the most influential philosophy. Within Confucianism, however, there were different traditions, from the philosophy of the classic Song and Ming Confucianism to the more modern ideas such as those of Kang Youwei.

Book of Changes

1

Book of Changes

THE *BOOK OF CHANGES* (*YIJING, I CHING,* OR *ZHOUYI*) is one of the oldest classics of China and was originally used for divination. The heart of the book consists of sixty-four cabalistic signs, called hexagrams. Each hexagram consists of a combination of six lines, which are either straight or broken. The first part of the *Book of Changes* presents the hexagrams and their meanings. It is assumed that this part existed as early as the eighth century BC.

The second part, the *Great Appendix* or the *Ten Wings,* consists of commentaries and remarks that were added later. But these are not just a treatise on the hexagrams. They explain the general meaning of the *Book of Changes.* The term *taiji* can be found here. *Taiji* represents the origin of the hexagrams and thus, from a philosophical point of view, the origin of all things and beings in the cosmos. (Please note: You will also find *taiji* written as Tai Chi, as in the name Tai Chi Chuan.) This early use of the term *taiji* is special because, in the philosophical literature of the classical period (before 220 BC), it is otherwise only found in the *Zhuangzi.*

After adding the *Great Appendix,* the *Book of Changes* was not only used for divination but gained a much more general significance. It was now used as an advisor for the ordering of human affairs in politics and society. Several parts of the *Book of Changes* were attributed directly to Confucius, and it was therefore entered in the *Five Classics (Wujing)* and became a central text of Confucianism. Because of its fundamental meaning for Chinese society, it is no wonder that we also find influences of the *Book of Changes* in Tai Chi Chuan. First of all, it structures the world in pairs of opposites generated by *taiji* and in the endless change between these pairs. These two ideas had a fundamental influence on Tai Chi Chuan.

In ancient times,
when the sages created the *Book of Changes,*
they followed the principle
of the inner nature *(xing)* and destiny.
Therefore, they established the way *(dao)* of heaven
and called it yin and yang.
Therefore, they established the way *(dao)* of earth
and called it hard and soft.
Therefore, they established the way *(dao)* of man
and called it humanity *(ren)* and righteousness.
They doubled these three powers
and therefore in the *Book of Changes*
six lines became a hexagram.

Heaven is high, earth is low.
Thus the creative and the receptive were determined.
With the explanation of high and low
noble and mean had their places assigned accordingly.
Movement and stillness received their constancy,
hard and soft were thus differentiated.

Once yin, once yang, this is the way *(dao)*.
What issues from it is goodness.
In completion it is called the inner nature *(xing)*
of all things and beings.
The man of humanity sees it
and calls it humanity *(ren)*.
The sage sees it
and calls it wisdom.
The common man acts according to it daily
but is not aware of it.

Thus, the way *(dao)* of the gentleman is rare.
It manifests itself in humanity *(ren)*
but conceals its workings.
It rouses the ten thousand things *(wanwu)*
without sharing the anxieties of the sage.
Its glorious inner power *(de)*
and its great achievement are supreme.
It fills everything with abundance,
thus is its great achievement.
It renews everything daily,

thus is its glorious inner power *(de)*.
Production and reproduction,
this is called change.

In the change is *taiji,*
which generates the two forms [yin and yang].
The two forms generate the four modes
and the four modes generate the eight trigrams *(bagua)*.

Confucius

孔
子

2

Confucius

CONFUCIUS (IN CHINESE, KONGZI) WAS BORN in 551 BC in the state of Lu, the descendant of lesser nobility. Because of the relative poverty in which he grew up, he was more or less self-taught. It is said that Confucius became the administrator of the granary of Lu at the age of twenty and that he started to teach not much later. Then he left Lu and traveled with his students to many states, offering his advice to the feudal lords. Thus he became the first "wandering" teacher, although not meeting with much success.

Confucius died in 479 BC without leaving any written work. The book in which his sayings are collected is called the *Analects (Lunyu,* also referred to as *Confucius)* and was written down after his death by his students. Although during his life Confucius had no success spreading his teaching, he became the pioneer for generations of scholars and philosophers.

In his teaching Confucius tried to give society a structure built on morals and rites. The order established through morals is represented by the word *ren,* which can be translated as "humanity." In the teachings of Confucius, humanity *(ren)* is the sum of human virtues, such as filial piety, trust, loyalty, altruism, and righteousness. Humanity *(ren)* is an inborn quality of human beings, but it has to be developed by learning and education. Therefore, the *Analects* contain intensive thoughts about learning. For Confucius, learning is the foundation for self-cultivation and a lifelong process that cannot be interrupted. In Tai Chi Chuan the student follows this idea. When one begins to learn Tai Chi Chuan, Confucius can become for the student what he has always been for the Chinese people—the Great Teacher.

Confucius said,
To learn and to repeat from time to time
what has been learned,
is this not a pleasure?
To have friends coming from afar,
is this not delightful?
Not to be recognized,
but not to feel hurt,
is one like this not a gentleman?

(BOOK I, VERSE 1)

Master Zeng said,
Three times a day I examine myself.
In acting on behalf of others,
have I always been loyal to their interests?
In my dealings with my friends,
have I always been true?

What has been handed down to me,
have I repeated it again and again?

(**I**, 4)

In practicing the rites,
harmony is of the highest order.
The way *(dao)* of the old kings
took its beauty from it.
It is the cause of great and small matters.
Yet this will not always work.
To know about harmony
but not regulate it by the rites,
this will not work.

(**I**, 12)

The Master said,
At fifteen I set my mind on learning.
At thirty I took my stand.
At forty I had no more perplexities.
At fifty I understood the will of heaven.
At sixty I was able to follow with my ears.
At seventy I was able to follow my heart's desire
without overstepping the boundaries.

(**II**, 4)

The Master said,
Review the old and gain knowledge of the new.
Thus one is fit to be a teacher.

(**II**, 11)

The Master said,
Learning without thinking,
this is bewildering.
Thinking without learning,
this is dangerous.

(**II**, 15)

The Master said,
In archery the main point is not
to pierce the middle,
for the reason that strength varies
from man to man.
This is the way *(dao)* of the ancestors.

(**III**, 16)

Zigong said,
What I do not want others to do to me,
I do not want to do to them.

(**V**, 12)

When Zilu heard something
that he had not put into practice,
his one fear was
that he might hear something more.

(**V**, 13)

The Master said,
To know of something is not as good
as to be fond of it.

To be fond of something is not as good
as to find joy in it.

(VI, 20)

The Master said,
The mean as an inner power *(de)* is supreme.
It is rarely found among the common people.

(VI, 27)

The Master said,
To be silent and store up knowledge,
learning without flagging,
to teach others without getting tired,
this is my way.

(VII, 2)

The Master said,
The thought
that the inner power *(de)* is not cultivated,
that learning is not taken seriously,
that one has heard of the right,
but does not move toward it,
that wrongs are not being changed,
this causes me concern.

(VII, 3)

The Master said,
Set your heart upon the way *(dao)*.
Support yourself by the inner power *(de)*,

lean upon humanity *(ren)*,
and cultivate the arts.

(**VII**, 6)

The Master said,
If one does not burst with eagerness,
I do not teach him.
If one is not trying to put his ideas into words,
I do not help him in his development.
If I show one corner to someone,
and he is not able to transfer it to the other three,
I will not repeat it.

(**VII**, 8)

Master Zeng said,
Gifted, and yet ask those
who are not gifted.
Possessing much, and yet ask those
who possess little.
Having, but yet appear not to have.
Full *(shi)*, but appearing empty *(xu)*.
Attacked, but not contesting.
Long ago I had a friend,
whose ways were such as this.

(**VIII**, 5)

Learn, as if you can't reach up to it,
as though you were frightened
to lose it.

(**VIII**, 17)

Yan Hui said with a deep sigh,
The more I look up, the higher it appears.
The more I bore into it, the harder it seems.
I see it before me and suddenly it is behind me.
The Master is guiding the people step by step.
He broadened me with the cultural *(wen)*.
He restrained me with the rites.
Yet though I wanted to give it up, I cannot.
Yet though I exhausted all my power,
it seems to rise above me.
Yet though I want to go after it,
there is no way.

(IX, 10)

The Master said,
As in the case of a mound,
if it is raised till only one more basketful is needed
and then is interrupted,
this is a standstill for me.
As in the case of starting with level ground,
if only one basketful is tilted,
this is progress for me.

(IX, 19)

Ordering by non-action *(wuwei)*,
thus was Shun.

(XV, 5)

Laozi

3

Laozi

Laozi (also spelled Lao Tzu), in Chinese, means "Old Master." Besides Confucius, he is one of the best-known thinkers of Chinese philosophy. In contrast to Confucius, little is known about Laozi's life, and some people assume that he did not exist at all. The most famous story about Laozi relates that he was an archivist at the court of the Zhou in the sixth century BC. Discontented with the government, he left his post and rode an ox through the country. When he was crossing the Hangu Pass the guard of the pass, Yin Xi, asked him to leave a written record. He agreed, and wrote straight away the *Daodejing* (or *Tao Te Ching*), which is commonly known as the *Laozi*. Then he continued on his journey and nobody knows what happened to him.

The *Daodejing* is of definitive importance in Chinese philosophy. Laozi extends here the meaning of the term "way" *(dao)* fundamentally. On the one hand, the way *(dao)* becomes the general principle of the cosmos. On the other, the way *(dao)* is something that can be approached by meditation. It is an ethical principle, based on insight into the natural cause of things.

Besides the way *(dao),* the term *de* is one of the key concepts of Laozi. The original meaning of *de* was "power" or "ability." In the *Laozi, de* is an inner power that comes from the way *(dao)* and that acts through the principle of non-action *(wuwei).* In Confucianism, *de* is the moral power of a human being, which is often translated as "virtue."

Laozi is known as the master of the teaching of the opposites. The introduction of these principles to solve situations of conflict had a deep influence on Tai Chi Chuan. As in the *Laozi,* in Tai Chi Chuan one prefers to yield and to be soft. The deep self-knowledge and the development of an inner power that is necessary for this is an important point in the *Laozi* and in Tai Chi Chuan. When one attains this ability, one can guide situations of conflict at an early stage and a solution will come naturally.

> He who knows others is wise.
> He who knows himself is enlightened.
> He who conquers others has strength.
> He who conquers himself is strong.
> He who is content is rich.
> He who acts with vigor has will.
> He who does not lose his place will endure.
> He who dies, but is not forgotten, lives forever.
>
> (VERSE 33)

What is to be contracted
must first be stretched.
What is to be weakened
must first be made strong.
What is to let fall
must first be lifted.
What is to be taken
must first be given.
This is called understanding the deep.
The soft overcomes the hard.
The weak overcomes the strong.
The fish should not leave the deep water.
Sharp weapons of the state should not be displayed
to the people.

(36)

The softest in the world overcomes the hardest in the
    world.
The non-being penetrates where there is no space.
Through this I know of the value of non-action *(wuwei)*.
Teaching without words.
Value the non-action *(wuwei)*.
Few in the world reach this.

(43)

What is still is easy to hold.
What is not yet manifested is easy to guide.
What is brittle is easy to crack.

What is minute is easy to scatter.

Deal with things before they appear.

Order things before they become confused.

The mighty tree began as a tiny sprout.

The tower nine stories high began with a heap of earth.

A journey of a thousand miles starts with one step.

He who acts, harms.

He who grabs, loses.

Therefore, the sage does not act and so does not harm.

He does not grab and so does not lose.

The people in their tasks, when they are about to
    succeed, spoil it.

Heed the end no less than the beginning

and it will not be spoiled.

Therefore, the sage desires not to desire.

He does not want rare things.

Learns not to learn.

Regains what the people have lost.

Thus he supports the ten thousand things *(wanwu)*

to be natural *(ziran),*

but dares not to act.

(64)

A skillful general is not martial *(wu).*

A skillful fighter is not angry.

A skillful conqueror is not competitive.

A skillful leader of the people puts himself below them.

This is the inner power *(de)* of not-competing.

This is the strength of leading men.
This means matching the highest of heaven.

(68)

For the use of fighters there is a saying:
I do not dare to be the host, I prefer to be the guest.
I do not dare to advance an inch, I prefer to retreat one
　　foot.
This is a march without marching.
Resist without arms.
Subdue without fighting.
Act without arms.
There is no greater danger than taking the enemy too
　　lightly.
To take the enemy lightly is the losing of my treasures.
Therefore, where two equal enemies meet,
he who is sorry about the fact will win.

(69)

Nothing in the world is softer and weaker than water,
but in attacking the hard and strong there is nothing
　　which outdoes it.
It is easy for it because of its non-being.
The weak overcomes the strong.
The soft overcomes the hard.
This is known by everyone,
but none practices it.
Therefore, the sage says,

Only he who has accepted the dirt of the country
can be lord of the shrines.
Only he who takes upon himself the country's
    misfortunes
can become the king of the world.
True words are like their opposite.

                                         (78)

Sunzi

孫

子

4

Sunzi

IN TRADITIONAL CHINESE THINKING, WAR WAS always regarded with skepticism. Nevertheless, it plays a significant role in classical Chinese philosophy. Nearly all great philosophers dealt with this topic. This is in line with the traditional Chinese concept that there should be no separation between theory and practice in philosophy. For the practice of warfare this means that one must follow the laws of the cosmos as recognized by philosophy. Only by insight into these laws can warfare become successful.

Parallel with the philosophers in old China who speculated upon warfare, military strategists exercised their handicraft in the service of a ruler on the basis of philosophical understanding. The writings of these military strategists are also classified in China under philosophy, as in the imperial catalogue *The History of the Han Dynasty*.

The greatest and best known of these strategists is Sunzi (also spelled Sun Tzu; full name Sun Wu). He was a contemporary of Confucius and left the work *Master Sun: The Art of War (Sunzi Bingfa)*. If the philosopher Laozi is considered master of the theory of opposites, the strategist Sunzi is master of its application in warfare. His whole work is permeated by this thought. As martial artists, most great Tai Chi Chuan masters had close contacts with the military. So it can be assumed that they studied the work of Sunzi intensively. It is no surprise, then, that the strategy of Tai Chi Chuan seems so similar to that of Sunzi.

Sunzi said,
War is a vital matter of the State,
a matter of life and death
and the way *(dao)* to survival or extinction.
Therefore, it must be examined with the greatest care.

Warfare is the way *(dao)* of deception.
Thus, if you are ready, seem not ready.
If you are close, seem far away.
If you are far away, seem close.
If the other one is at an advantage, entice him.
If he is in disorder, take him.
If he is full *(shi)*, be prepared.
If he is strong, evade him.
If he is angry, give way to him.
If he is holding back, look arrogant.
If he is rested, molest him.
If he is united, split him.

Attack where he is not prepared.
Go forth where it would never occur to him.

The art of war is this:
It is better to keep your own country intact
than to destroy the other's.
It is better to keep your own army intact
than to destroy the other's.
It is better to keep your own battalion,
company, or five-man squad intact
than to destroy the other's.
Thus, to win a hundred victories in a hundred battles
is not the pinnacle of excellence.
To subdue the other without fighting,
that is the pinnacle of excellence.

He who knows the other and himself
will never be at risk in a hundred battles.
He who does not know the other, but himself,
will once win and once lose.
He who does not know the other, or himself,
will lose every battle.

If the enemy makes preparations at the front,
he will weaken his back.
If the enemy makes preparations at the back,
he will weaken his front.
If the enemy makes preparations at the left,

he will weaken his right.
If the enemy makes preparations at the right,
he will weaken his left.
If the enemy makes preparations everywhere,
he will be weak everywhere.

The positioning of the army is like unto water.
Water runs away from high places and hastens
    downward.
So in the positioning of the army one avoids the full *(shi)*
and strikes into the empty *(xu)*.
Water follows in its flow the nature of the ground.
An army that acts according to the enemy will gain
    victory in this way.
As an army has no constant power,
so water retains no constant shape.
If you are acting according to the enemy,
the transformation and the victory will be miraculous.

Zhuangzi

莊

子

5

Zhuangzi

ZHUANGZI, CONSIDERED THE SECOND GREAT DAOIST, is an unusually interesting philosopher. He probably lived around 350 BC, although the exact dates are not known. It is said that he was very modest and that he frequently rejected high office. The book *Zhuangzi* (published originally as *The True Book of the Southern Flower Country*) was probably partially written by Zhuangzi himself. In contrast to the often mysterious sayings of the *Laozi*, it contains humorous stories, parables, and anecdotes.

An important concept in *Zhuangzi* is non-acting *(wuwei)*, which means neither too much nor too little action. One who is able to attain this approaches the way *(dao)* and becomes a true human. True humans are characterized by their calm and empty spirit, do not live for the outside world, and can complete their full lifespan. In Tai Chi Chuan these thoughts are also of great importance. *Zhuangzi,* as one of the pillars of Chinese philosophy, is an absolute must for all students of Tai Chi Chuan.

I have heard
of letting the world be
and letting the world alone.
I have never heard
of regulating the world.
Letting the world be means to fear
that it will go beyond its inner nature *(xing)*.
Letting the world alone means to fear
that it changes its inner power *(de)*.
If the world does not go beyond its inner nature *(xing)*
or change its inner power *(de)*,
what need is there to regulate the world?
In ancient times, when King Yao regulated the world,
he made everybody extremely happy,
enjoying their inner nature *(xing)*.
So there was no stillness anymore.
When King Jie regulated the world,
he made everybody fully exhausted,
harming their inner nature *(xing)*.
So there was no pleasure any longer.
To be without stillness and pleasure
is the opposite of the inner power *(de)*.
To abide long without inner power *(de)*
is not possible.
Who is too happy
will reach the limit of yang.
Who is too exhausted
will reach the limit of yin.

(FROM **Chapter** 11)

~ *34* ~

Man's life is limited.
Knowledge is unlimited.
To pursue what is unlimited with what is limited
is a perilous thing.
To know this and still seek for knowledge
is even more perilous.
When you do good,
fame does not have to be close.
When you do evil,
punishment does not have to be close.
Who is in accordance with what is handed down
will preserve his body,
maintain his life, nourish his relations,
and complete his full lifespan.

(FROM CHAPTER 3)

Nanbo Ziqi was wandering in Shangqiu when he saw a huge tree of quite extraordinary size. The teams of a thousand chariots could be sheltered under it. Ziqi said, "What kind of a tree is this? It must be of unusual timber."

Looking up he saw its smaller branches. They were so twisted that they could not be made into beams. Looking down he saw its roots. They were so knobby that no coffin could be made of them. When you licked one of its leaves, your mouth felt torn and wounded. When you smelled it, you were intoxicated for three days. Ziqi said, "This tree is good for nothing. And it is because of this that it attained such a size. Ah, the sage, he is like this, worthless."

(FROM CHAPTER 4)

When Tian Kaizhi visited Duke Wei of Zhou, the duke said, "I have heard that Zhu Shen studied the art of life. You, master, who knew him, what have you heard him saying about it?"

Tian Kaizhi said, "I have only swept with a broom in front of his gate. What should I have heard?"

The duke said, "Please don't be modest. We really want to hear about it."

Tian Kaizhi said, "I have heard my master saying: 'Nourishing one's life *(yangsheng)* is like taking care of sheep. If you see some lagging behind, you use the whip to urge them on.'"

The duke asked, "What does that mean?"

Tian Kaizhi said, "In Lu there was a man named Shan Bao. He lived in a cave, drank water, was not looking for profit, and still looked like a little child. Unfortunately, he encountered a hungry tiger, which killed and ate him. There was also a man named Zhang Yi. He was a favorite among the rich and the poor alike. At the age of forty, he died of an inner fever. Shan Bao cultivated his inner, but a tiger ate his outer. Zhang Yi cultivated his outer, but a disease attacked his inner. Neither of the two attended to their lagging qualities."

(FROM CHAPTER 19)

Ji Shengzi raised a gamecock for the king. After ten days the king asked, "Is the cock ready for fighting?"

Ji said, "Not yet. He is still proud and arrogant."

After a further ten days, the king asked again and Ji said, "Not yet. He still reacts to sounds and to the sight of the surroundings."

After a further ten days, the king asked again and Ji said, "Not yet. He still has the error of unsteady view and of vanity."

After a further ten days, the king asked again and Ji said, "Now he is ready. Even if other cocks crow, he will not be affected by it. At first sight he appears like a cock made of wood. His inner power *(de)* is completed. Other cocks do not dare to provoke him. They turn and run away."

(FROM CHAPTER 19)

Many years ago King Wen from Zhao enjoyed the art of swordplay so much that within his gates were more than three thousand swordfighters. They fought day and night before him and, even though in one year more than one hundred were mortally wounded, the king's fondness for swordplay never faded. After three years the country began to decline and the nobles began to conspire.

The crown prince was very worried and spoke to the officials: "Whoever can persuade the king to give up his love of swordfighting gets a thousand gold coins."

The officials answered, "Zhuangzi can do this."

Immediately, the crown prince sent envoys to politely offer Zhuangzi a thousand gold coins. Zhuangzi rejected them, but followed the envoys to meet the crown prince and asked him, "What can I do for you that you offer so much gold to me?"

The crown prince answered, "I heard you are a wise master. The offer of a thousand gold coins was meant for your devoted followers. You, however, rejected it. What more can I say?"

Zhuangzi said, "I heard that the crown prince would like me to persuade the king to abandon his passion. If my words displease the king and the crown prince, then I will be punished and killed. Why should gold make such an offer appealing to me? If my words are accepted, however, by the king and the crown prince, then in the Kingdom of Zhao there is nothing that I could not ask for."

The crown prince answered, "That is true, but the king only likes to see swordfighters."

Zhuangzi said, "Yes, certainly, but I am also good at swordfighting."

The crown prince said, "However, the swordfighters the king wants to see have tousled hair, wild curls, down-hanging hats, unkempt hat ribbons, short clothes, glaring expressions, and insulting language. The king only likes it that way. If you meet the king in a scholar's robe, you will fail."

Zhuangzi said, "Please bring me the clothes of a swordfighter."

Three days later, after he had received the clothes of a swordfighter, Zhuangzi met the crown prince. The crown prince went to see the king with him. The king waited for them with his sword unsheathed. Zhuangzi went without hurrying into the palace and stepped without prostrating in front of the king.

The king asked, "What do you want to teach us, that you need to be introduced by the crown prince?"

Zhuangzi said, "Your servant heard that you are very fond of the art of swordplay. Therefore, I would like to show you my art of swordplay."

The king asked, "How do you use your sword to strike the opponent?"

Zhuangzi said, "The art of the sword of your servant can defeat one opponent every ten paces. Over a thousand miles, none can resist."

The king was pleased: "Then there is nowhere an enemy for you."

Zhuangzi said, "In my art of swordplay I show my emptiness *(xu)* and let the other take the advantage. Afterward I attack and strike first. I would like to try it here once."

The king said, "We would like to rest somewhat. Wait for my instructions. We will arrange a match and invite you, too."

The king had the swordfighters compete for seven days. Sixty were hurt or killed. Five or six of the fighters were asked to come with their swords in front of the palace. Then Zhuangzi was called.

The king said, "Today I invite you to compete with these fighters."

Zhuangzi said, "I am ready for this."

The king asked, "Will you defend yourself with a long or a short sword?"

Zhuangzi said, "All swords are fine for your servant. But I have three swords and you should decide which I am to use. First, I would like to explain what I mean. Afterward I will fight."

The king said, "Let us hear of these three swords."

Zhuangzi said, "I have the sword of the emperor, the sword of the feudal lord, and the sword of the common man."

The king asked, "What is the sword of the emperor?"

Zhuangzi said, "The sword of the emperor has the Yanxi ravines and the Shicheng mountains as the point. The mountain Tai in Qi as the blade. The realms of Jin and Wei as the spine. The realms of Zhou and Song as the ring. The realms of Han and Wei as the handle. It is wrapped with the four tribes at the borders of the realm and the four seasons. Enclosed by the Bohai sea. Surrounded with the Heng mountains. It prevails by the five phases *(wuxing)* and executes by punishment and goodness. It unfolds through yin and yang, stays by spring and summer and changes by autumn and winter. Nothing remains in front of this sword, whether from above, down, or from the side. Above like clouds flowing. Down the earth splitting. If this sword is pulled, lords are controlled and the whole world is the subject. That is the sword of the emperor."

Surprised, the king asked, "What is the sword of the feudal lord?"

Zhuangzi said, "The sword of the feudal lord has men of intelligence and bravery as the point. Men of honesty as the blade. Men of virtue and excellence as the spine. Men of loyalty and wisdom as the ring and men of valor as the handle. Also nothing remains in front of this sword, whether from above, down, or from the side. Above like the law of the round heaven. The sun, the moon, and the stars following. Down like the law of the square earth. The four seasons following. In the center is harmony with the will of the people and peace develops in the country. If this sword is pulled, it shakes like loud thunder. Within the four directions there is nobody who would not follow the instructions of the ruler. That is the sword of the feudal lord."

The king asked, "And the sword of the common man?"

Zhuangzi said, "The sword of the common man is carried by people with tousled hair, wild curls, down-hanging hats, unkempt hat ribbons, short clothes, glaring expressions, and insulting language. They fight for the public, cutting each other's heads off or piercing each other in liver and lung. That is the sword of the common man. He is like a gamecock. Once he dies, he is of no use to the state. Your majesty has the rank of an emperor, but loves the sword of the common man. In the opinion of your servant, this is without dignity for his majesty."

The king led Zhuangzi into the palace, ordered meals, and walked three times in a circle.

Zhuangzi said, "Your majesty, please sit down and calm yourself. My report of the sword for you has finished."

Thereafter the king did not leave his palace for three months. The swordfighters, however, followed instructions and killed themselves.

(FROM CHAPTER 30)

Wuzi

6

Wuzi

THE STRATEGIST WUZI (CA. 440–381 BC) is generally recognized as the first great general of China. He fought often against overwhelming odds, but was never defeated. The book *Wuzi* was probably written by him, but it was published by his students as a summary of his strategic philosophy. In his book, Wuzi deals with how one can form a stable and durable state. He is of the opinion that civilian and military aspects of the government are of equivalent importance. Only if both are sufficiently considered can a state prosper. Furthermore, he explains how the military is to be led. He considers practical aspects, from war preparations to specific tactics in battle.

If one says of Sunzi that his thinking has Daoist roots, then, in contrast, Wuzi is the Confucian among the strategists. He says this also of himself. In the *Records of the Historian (Shiji),* it is written about the two that whenever military affairs were discussed, both names, Sunzi and Wuzi, were mentioned together.

Those who learn Tai Chi Chuan practice an old Chinese martial art. Nevertheless, most students of Tai Chi Chuan view the use of violence skeptically. This skepticism can also be found in the texts of the strategists of old China. Although they were responsible for warfare, they warn time and again that violence may be only the last of all means. Wuzi presents a good example of this.

> Wuzi says,
> The way *(dao)* is the means
> by which one turns back to the roots
> and returns to the original one.
> Righteousness is the means
> by which one acts correctly and earns achievements.
> Planning is the means
> by which one keeps harm distant and gains profit.
> Having a foundation is the means
> by which one protects the achieved and preserves
>   existence.
> If the actions are not in accord with the way *(dao)*
> and the behavior is not in accord with righteousness,
> then one may be high-ranking and noble,
> but misfortune will strike one nevertheless.
> Therefore, the sage pacifies the people with the way
>   *(dao),*
> regulates them with righteousness,
> moves them with the ritual,
> and pacifies them by humanity *(ren).*

If these four inner powers *(de)* are cultivated, one
    flourishes.
If they are ignored, decline follows.

To gain victory in war is easy,
but to retain the victory is difficult.
Therefore, it is said,
that the state in this world
which makes war and achieves five victories
will be stricken by misfortune.
That one which achieves four victories will be exhausted.
That one which achieves three victories becomes an
    occupying power.
That one which achieves two victories becomes king.
That one which achieves one victory becomes emperor.
Therefore, there are few who achieve a large number
    of victories in the world,
but many who perish.

To unite the cultural *(wen)* and the martial *(wu)* in
    oneself
is the task of the general.
To unite the hard and the soft in oneself
is the affair of the soldier.
Usually, when people discuss generalship,
they focus on courage.
But courage is only one of the characteristics of the
    general.

The courageous one will go thoughtlessly into the
    battle.
To go thoughtless into the battle
without knowing the advantages,
that does not work.

Inner Training

7

Inner Training

*I*NNER *TRAINING (NEIYE)* IS ONE OF the oldest Daoist texts on inner cultivation and is an important forerunner of the practice of nourishing one's life *(yangsheng)*. It is in a collection of texts called *Guanzi* that date from approximately 300 BC. However, the text itself seems to be much older.

Relying on Daoist cosmology, *Inner Training* provides guidance for the development of body and mind, nutrition, respiration, and application of the *qi.* The student is regarded as a whole and there is no strict separation of the physical and the mental. For example, the term "align" refers to the heart-mind *(xin)* and to the *qi,* but also to the body and the limbs.

The tradition of nourishing one's life *(yangsheng)* flowed into Tai Chi Chuan. Reading *Inner Training,* one sometimes has the impression of reading a Tai Chi classic. It is an exciting text with many suggestions for the practice of Tai Chi Chuan.

Only if one is aligned and still,
one can be stable.
A stable heart-mind *(xin)* is in the center,
eyes and ears sharp and clear,
the four limbs strong and firm.
Thus can one shelter the essence *(jing)*.
The essence *(jing)* is the refinement of the *qi*.
When the *qi* flows freely,
there is life.
When there is life,
there is thought.
When there is thought,
there is knowledge.
When there is knowledge,
one must stop.
When there is too much knowledge in the heart-mind
    (xin),
one loses his life.

When the body is not aligned,
the inner power *(de)* cannot develop.
When one is not still inside,
the heart-mind *(xin)* cannot be well ordered.
Align the body and pay attention to the inner power
    (de).
Thus one will gradually attain it.

When one is aligned and still,
the skin will be healthy and smooth.

Eyes and ears are sharp and clear.
Muscles are supple and the bones are hard.
So one can support the large circle [the heaven]
and step along the large square [the earth].
One reflects in great purity.
One appears in great clarity.

Exist carefully, without exaggeration.
Daily renew one's inner power *(de)*.
Know everything of this world.
Examine everything in the four directions.
Develop attentively one's abundance.
This is called "inward achievement."
If one does all this in this way, but does not return,
then this becomes too much.

About the way *(dao):*
One must encircle, one must pull together.
One must extend, one must stretch.
One must strengthen, one must be persistent.
Keep the precious and do not give it away.
Banish excess and abandon deficit.
As soon as one reaches the extreme,
one returns to the way *(dao)*
and to the inner power *(de)*.

About the life of humans:
Heaven gives the essence *(jing)*.
Earth gives the body.

Combined they make a person.
In harmony with each other they make life.
No harmony, no life.
If one examines the way *(dao)* of the harmony,
one cannot see its essence *(jing)*.
There are not many signs.
Balance and alignment are in one's mind.
Thus the way of harmony sinks
into the heart-mind *(xin)*
and one achieves a long life.

Great Learning

8

Great Learning

THE GREAT LEARNING (DAXUE) FIRST APPEARED in the first century BC in the Confucian *Book of the Rites (Liji)*. In the following centuries the *Great Learning* did not receive any special attention in Chinese philosophy. This changed with Zhu Xi, the great Neo-Confucian philosopher of the Song era (960–1279 AD). He worked intensively for years on the *Great Learning* and wrote a comment for each individual sentence. Thus it moved to the forefront of the Neo-Confucian philosophy. Together with the *Book of the Mean (Zhongyong)*, the *Analects,* and the *Mencius,* the *Great Learning* became one of the *Four Books (Sishu),* the classics of Neo-Confucianism.

In its philosophy the *Great Learning* outlines a central topic of the Confucian teaching in short and concise words: The correct structure of the society—the order in family and state, as well as peaceful and respectful dealings with each other—has its origin in the development of the personality of the individual. This becomes a fundamental process in Confucianism that is called self-cultivation. Traditionally in China the arts also serve as techniques of self-cultivation. Therefore, one can imagine that many masters of Tai Chi Chuan saw their art not only as a collection of self-defense techniques or health exercises but also as a form of self-cultivation. This also explains the great importance of the solo forms, which many students of Tai Chi Chuan consider to be the substance of their art.

The way *(dao)* of the great learning consists
of the clear and pure inner power *(de),* loving the people,
and in seeing one's goal as the highest good.
If one has knowledge of one's goal, one becomes firm.
If one is firm, one becomes still.
If one is still, one becomes composed.
If one is composed, one can think thoroughly.
If one thinks thoroughly, one will arrive.

Things have their roots and branches.
Affairs have their beginning and end.
He who knows what comes first and what follows after
is close to the way *(dao).*

The ancients who wanted to explain
their clear and pure inner power *(de)* to the world
would first bring order to their state.
To bring order to their state,
they would first regulate their family.
To regulate their family,
they would first cultivate themselves.

To cultivate themselves,
they would first rectify their heart-mind *(xin)*.
To rectify their heart-mind *(xin)*,
they first made their intentions *(yi)* sincere *(cheng)*.
To make their intentions *(yi)* sincere *(cheng)*,
they would first extend their knowledge.
The extension of knowledge lies in the investigation of
    things.

After things are investigated,
knowledge is extended.
After knowledge is extended,
the intentions *(yi)* become sincere *(cheng)*.
After the intentions *(yi)* are sincere *(cheng)*,
the heart-mind *(xin)* becomes still.
After the heart-mind *(xin)* is still,
the self is cultivated.
After the self is cultivated,
the family is regulated.
After the family is regulated,
the state is in order.
After the state is in order,
the whole world will find peace.

One says,
From the emperor to the common man,
all take self-cultivation as the root.
For the root to be in disorder,
but the branches to be in order,

that is impossible.
That the important is unimportant
and the unimportant is important,
that has never been the case.

Book of the Mean

9

Book of the Mean

THE *BOOK OF THE MEAN (ZHONGYONG)* is often spoken of in the same breath as the *Great Learning (Daxue)*. It is also part of the *Book of the Rites (Liji)* and was included as one of the *Four Books (Sishu)* of Confucianism. This shows its great importance in Chinese culture. While the *Great Learning* describes social and political aspects, psychological and metaphysical topics are important in the *Book of the Mean,* thus forming a bridge from Confucianism to Daoists and Buddhists, who also felt strongly attracted to this book.

As the title of the book suggests, the term "mean" is of special importance. The mean is understood as a moral state in which extreme emotions are avoided. The actions of humans who stay with the mean will correspond to the principles of the cosmos. A further important term is "sincerity" *(cheng)*. Sincerity *(cheng)* reaches beyond the human world. All things and the way *(dao)* of heaven can be sincere *(cheng)*. Sincerity *(cheng)* means to follow one's inner nature *(xing)* and could therefore be translated also as "authentic" or "genuine." The old Tai Chi Chuan masters demanded adherence to the mean and sincerity *(cheng)* from their students.

> What heaven assigns is the inner nature *(xing)*.
> What the inner nature *(xing)* prescribes is called the
>   way *(dao)*.
> What makes cultivation toward the way *(dao)* possible
>   is called education.
> The way *(dao)* may not be left for one moment.
> If one could leave it, it would not be the way *(dao)*.

> Therefore, the gentleman pays attention to what he
>   does not see
> and is careful about what he does not hear.
> There is nothing more visible than the hidden.
> There is nothing clearer than the invisible.
> Therefore, the gentleman is watchful over himself.

> If luck and anger, sorrow and joy are not yet aroused,
> one calls this the mean.
> If they are present, but in correct rhythm,
> one calls this harmony.
> The mean is the large root of the world.
> Harmony means to fulfill the way *(dao)*.
> If the mean and harmony are attained,
> then heaven and earth *(tiandi)* have their place
> and the ten thousand things *(wanwu)* will flourish.

The master says,
The mean is of highest importance,
but the man who stays there is rare.

Sincerity *(cheng)* is the way *(dao)* of heaven.
To strive for sincerity *(cheng)* is the way *(dao)* of man.

Sincerity *(cheng)* is to keep the mean without effort.
Reaching without thinking.
To walk with ease in the middle of the way *(dao)*.
Such is the sage.

To strive for sincerity *(cheng)* is
to choose the good and to keep it.
Learn comprehensively. Analyze thoroughly.
Think carefully. Examine clearly.
Carry out what you must do.

If there is something that one has not yet learned,
or something that one has learned,
but not yet mastered,
then one should not let go of it.

If there is something that one has not yet analyzed,
or something that one has analyzed,
but not yet understood,
then one should not let go of it.

If there is something that one has not yet thought about,
or something that one has thought about,
but not yet looked through,
then one should not let go of it.

If there is something that one has not yet examined,
or something that one has examined,
but not yet clarified,
then one should not let go of it.

If there is something that one has not yet done,
or something that one has done,
but has not yet completed,
then one should not let go of it.

If others can do it after the first time,
then I do it a hundred times.
If others can do it after the tenth time,
then I do it a thousand times.
If one follows this way *(dao)*,
then even the stupid one becomes intelligent
and the weak one becomes strong.

Sun Bin

孫臏

10

Sun Bin

SUN BIN, A DESCENDANT OF SUNZI, lived in 380–316 BC, more than a century after Sunzi. Like his ancestor, Sun Bin left a work called *Sun Bin: The Art of War (Sun Bin Bingfa)*. To better distinguish the two works, one speaks simply of the *Sunzi* (the work of Sun Wu) and the *Sun Bin* (the work of Sun Bin). The book *Sun Bin* was lost for nearly 2,000 years and was only rediscovered in a grave in 1972. Today it is considered one of the important texts of classical Chinese military philosophy.

In the previous chapter on Sunzi, we considered the principle of the opposites in strategic thinking. This thought is extended in Chinese philosophy as a dynamic process. When something exceeds its maximum, it turns into its opposite. One has only to think of the yin-yang symbol, in which a black point is already present in the large white part, and a white point present in the black part. In the *Sun Bin* this concept is also introduced to strategic thinking. Because the text was lost for two millennia, it was almost certainly not studied by Tai

Chi Chuan masters. But the clear formulation of this principle in a text this old shows how early it was integrated into Chinese strategic thinking. It is not surprising that it also serves as a foundation of Tai Chi Chuan.

The principle of heaven and earth *(tiandi)*:
When something reaches its maximum,
it returns.
When something is completely filled,
it empties again.
The changes between ascent and descent
are like the four seasons.
Victories and defeats
are like the five phases *(wuxing)*.
Life and death
are like the ten thousand things *(wanwu)*.
Able and unable
are like the ten thousand life-forms.
Somewhat more and somewhat less
are like the form and the power.

Therefore, he who is excellent in warfare
knows the weakness of the enemy
if he sees his strength.
He knows his deficiency
if he sees his abundance.
He sees the victory as clearly
as he sees the sun and the moon.

Sun Bin

He will triumph as surely
as water defeats fire.

One looks still,
in order to surprise with movement.
One looks comfortable,
in order to surprise by annoyance.
One looks satisfied,
in order to surprise with ambition.
One looks proper,
in order to surprise with disorder.
One looks numerous,
in order to surprise with a few.

Huainanzi

11

Huainanzi

THE BOOK *HUAINANZI* WAS COMPILED BY Liu An (179–122 BC), a grandchild of the first Han emperor, with the assistance of a group of scholars. Its central ideas follow the Daoist tradition of the *Laozi* and the *Zhuangzi*. As a political signpost it was directed against the increasing Confucianist centralism of the emperor's court. In its place, the *Huainanzi* presents an ideal feudal society, shaped by change. The term "change" refers to social, political, and cultural aspects, and to the surrounding nature. A central question in the *Huainanzi* thus is how one should position oneself in an eternally changing world. Liu An's ideas were not accepted at the emperor's court. He was later accused of betrayal and then committed suicide.

The *Huainanzi* of Liu An is of great interest for the student of Tai Chi Chuan. It describes in detail the Daoist cosmology on which Tai Chi Chuan is based. Many older ideas are taken up and explained more completely, such as the concept of correct timing, which is also familiar to students of Tai Chi Chuan.

> As for the way *(dao)*,
> It protects the heaven and supports the earth.
> It exceeds the four directions and opens the eight poles.
> It is endlessly large and boundlessly deep.
> It envelops heaven and earth *(tiandi)*
> and gives form to what has no form.
> Its origin and its run is like a spring.
> First empty, it becomes gradually full.
> Turbidly flowing, what is dark becomes slowly clear.

> One who understood the way *(dao)*
> turns back to clarity and stillness.
> One who examined everything
> ends with non-action *(wuwei)*.

> One who has attained the way *(dao)*
> is weak in his ideas, but strong in his actions.
> His heart-mind *(xin)* is empty *(xu)*,
> but his actions are rich.
> What does it mean to be weak in his ideas?
> One is soft and still.
> One hides behind shyness.
> One does what is not accepted,
> carelessly and without thinking.
> One moves, but not at too early a time.

Freewheeling, one turns to the ten thousand things
   (wanwu).
One does not take the lead
and one is only internally moved
when affected from the outside.

Therefore, he who wants to be hard must hold on to
   softness.
He who wants to be strong must protect himself by
   weakness.
Accumulating softness leads to hardness.
Accumulating weakness leads to strength.
Observe what is accumulated,
in order to recognize the direction of success and failing.
The hard overcomes what is not as hard as itself.
If it meets an equivalent hardness, neither wins.
The soft overcomes what is superior to it.
Its power is immeasurable.

Therefore, a weapon that is too rigid will burst.
A piece of wood that is too hard will break.
A piece of leather that is too brittle will tear.
The teeth, harder than the tongue, suffer the first damage.
Therefore, the soft and weak are the trunk of the life.
The hard and strong are the students of death.

One must keep the principle of the way *(dao)*
in order to follow the changes.

The earlier controls thus likewise the later,
as the later controls the earlier.
Why is it like that?
Since one never loses control over the others,
the others cannot control one.
The right moment is already gone,
before one took a breath.
The one who is too early has easily done too much.
The one who is too late has difficulty acting at all.
Sun and moon turn on their courses.
The right moment waits for no one.
Therefore, the sage values a little bit of time more than
     a piece of jade.
The right moment is difficult to reach but easy to miss.

Liezi

列子

12

Liezi

T HE BOOK *LIEZI* BELONGS TO THE Daoist tradition. Its reput-
ed author, Master Lie, lived between 450 and 375 BC. It
is, however, unlikely that he wrote the book. Literary-scientific
investigations indicate that it was compiled in the third century
AD and thus is part of Neo-Daoism. In content and style, the
book is very similar to the *Zhuangzi.*

Like the *Zhuangzi,* the thoughts in the *Liezi* are developed in
anecdotes and stories. Some of these anecdotes describe what it
means from the Daoist point of view to learn an art. The book
demands that the student trains regularly in the same elements
over a long period of time. Exercise thus becomes part of one's
being. In this way, great ability results completely naturally
from an intuitive accordance with the nature of the art. The
ability attained is, however, not used for showing off. Concepts
of this kind had a substantial effect on Tai Chi Chuan.

Confucius walked to Chu. As he came out of a small forest, he saw a hunchback who caught cicadas as if he only needed to pick them. Zhong Ni [another name for Confucius] asked, "Master, is there a way *(dao)* for your skill?"

The hunchback answered, "I have a way *(dao)*. For five or six months I balanced two balls on a rope, until they did not fall down any longer. Afterward, I missed only each sixth cicada. After I was able to do thus with three balls, I missed only one of ten. Finally, when I could do thus with five balls and not let them fall, I could simply pick the cicadas. I stand still, like a strong trunk. I keep my arms calm, like thick branches. From the ten thousand things *(wanwu)* between heaven and earth *(tiandi)*, I know only the wings of the cicadas. From those I do not turn away. I do not exchange the ten thousand things *(wanwu)* for the wings of the cicadas."

Confucius turned to his students and said, "Only one who can use his thoughts undivided can concentrate the spirit *(shen)* fully. That is what the hunchback wanted to say."

The hunchback said, "You in the robes, what do you know? First act, and then speak about it."

(BOOK II, CHAPTER 10)

Count Gong Yi was among the princes renowned for his power. Tang Xi told King Xuan of Zhou about Gong Yi. The king let gifts be prepared and invited Gong Yi. Gong Yi came, but appeared to be completely weak. The king was astonished and asked doubtfully, "How great is your power?"

Gong Yi answered, "The power of your subject is enough to break the leg of a spring grasshopper or to carry the wing of an autumn cicada."

The king turned red and said, "My strongest men can tear up the skin of a rhinoceros or pull nine bulls around by their tails. And they are still too weak for me. You, however, can break the leg of a spring grasshopper and carry the wing of an autumn cicada, but nevertheless everywhere one hears of your power. How can this be?"

Count Gong Yi breathed deeply, then rose up and said, "Oh, what a question, my king. I will dare to answer how this is. The teacher of your subject was Shang Qiuzi. Nobody was able to resist his power. But even his nearest relatives did not know anything about it since he would never use his power. When he was close to death, he said to me, 'People like to see what is not visible. However, they do not want to see the obvious. People like to attain what is not attainable. But they do not like to cultivate themselves. Therefore, who wants to learn to see should first just look at a cart full of firewood. Who wants to learn to hear should first just listen to the sound of a bell. Who is inside light knows outside nothing heavy. Who knows outside nothing heavy will not be known outside his family.' Today the name of your subject was heard by the princes. That shows that your subject did not follow the teachings of his master and has revealed his abilities. But the name of your subject is not based on the fact that he abuses his power, but that he can use it. Is that not much better than abusing his power?"

(IV, 12)

In the old days Gan Ying was an outstanding archer. Whenever he stretched his bow, wild animals collapsed and birds fell down. Gan Ying had a student by the name of Fei Wei, who exceeded even him in archery. Another man, Ji Chang, wanted to learn archery from Fei Wei. Fei Wei said, "First you must learn not to blink. Only then can we talk about archery."

Ji Chang went home, lay down under the loom of his wife, and fixed his eyes on the movements. After two years he did not blink anymore, even if an awl with its point fell into the angle of his eye. This he reported to Fei Wei. Fei Wei, however, said, "That is not yet enough. You must still learn to look, so that you can see the small as if it were large, and the indistinct as if it were clear. Then you can come back and tell me."

Ji Chang hung a louse on a hair in a window and looked at it. After ten days it became slowly larger. After three years it was as large as a cartwheel and in such a way all other things looked like mountains to him. So he took a bow made from horn of Yan and an arrow made from wood of Shuo and shot into the heart of the louse, without cutting the hair. Then he went to Fei Wei and reported this to him. Fei Wei jumped into the air, struck himself on the chest, and said, "Now you have got it."

As Ji Chang mastered the art in this way completely, he recognized that there was only one enemy for him in the whole world, and he decided to kill Fei Wei. They met in the wilderness and shot at each other. The tips of the arrows met in the middle between them and fell down, without stirring up dust. Fei Wei ran out of arrows first, but Ji Chang still had one. He shot it. Fei Wei repelled it with the thorn of a tree, without missing it. Then the two began to cry. They let their bows fall, bowed to the ground before each other full of respect, and became as father and son. They made cuts in their arms and swore to pass their art on to nobody.

(**V**, 15)

Glossary

名詞

Glossary

The cultural *(wen)*. The character *wen* refers, strictly speaking, to Chinese writing and literature. In the broader sense, however, it encompasses all the different cultural attributes, such as art, music, and rituals, all of which have a highly moral content. The cultural *(wen)* was the yardstick of the Confucianist "gentleman" (as the term *junzi* might best be translated, or as "superior man" or "exemplary person") in traditional China, an indication of true cultivation. Thus *wen* stands in opposition to the martial *(wu)*. The pair of terms *wen* and *wu*, and thus the relationship between the cultural and martial, or the civil and the military, form a topic that has been a matter of fervent debate in China. In Tai Chi Chuan one tries to develop harmony between the cultural *(wen)* and the martial *(wu)*.

cheng. See Sincerity.

dao. See Way.

de. See Inner power.

Eight trigrams *(bagua).* The eight trigrams *(bagua)* are cabalistic signs consisting of three lines lying one above the other. The lines are either solid (hard) or interrupted (soft). In general terminology one says that the hard lines represent yang and the soft lines yin. Allegedly, the eight trigrams were derived by the legendary emperor Fu Xi from his observations of nature. In Tai Chi Chuan the eight trigrams are assigned to the eight directions and the eight hand techniques *peng, lü, ji, an, cai, lie, zhou,* and *kao.*

Empty *(xu).* See Full *(shi).*

Essence *(jing).* Literally, fine. The essence *(jing)* stands for a kind of fine basic substance that circulates in humans and gives them their tangible form. In addition, the essence *(jing)* can be understood as the male and female sexual fluids. In Daoism, essence *(jing), qi,* and spirit *(shen)* form the three treasures. The refinement of the three treasures serves in Daoism as the foundation for the extension of life. In Tai Chi Chuan the three treasures are maintained by the development of naturalness *(ziran).*

Five Classics (Wujing). Since the Han Dynasty (206 BC–220 AD) one has spoken of the *Five Classics (Wujing)* of Confucianism. These are the *Spring and Autumn Annals (Chunqiu),* the *Rites (Yili),* the *Book of Odes (Shijing),* the *Book of History (Shujing),* and the *Book of Changes (Yijing).*

Five phases *(wuxing)*. Literally, the five travelers. These were known in antiquity as the five planets and the elements associated with them: water, fire, wood, metal, and earth. The five phases *(wuxing)* are assigned traditionally to the most different conditions in the micro- and macrocosm. In Tai Chi Chuan the five phases *(wuxing)* correspond to the five moves: advance, retreat, look left, look right, and central equilibrium.

Four Books (Sishu). The *Four Books (Sishu)* are the *Great Learning (Daxue),* the *Book of the Mean (Zhongyong),* the *Analects (Lunyu),* and the *Mencius.* They were arranged, annotated, and adopted as the new classic of Confucianism by the philosopher Zhu Xi in the Song Dynasty (960–1279 AD). In this form they became the standard for the training of officials until 1911.

Full *(shi)* and empty *(xu)*. Full *(shi)* and empty *(xu)* are a classic yin-yang pair. One can translate them also as "substantial" and "insubstantial." The concept of a yin-yang pair implies that something is not full *(shi)* or empty *(xu)*, but that both aspects are present at the same time and that these form an eternal cycle with each other. Both in the strategists' and in the Tai Chi Chuan literature, full *(shi)* and empty *(xu)* play an important part. With reference to the heart-mind *(xin)*, emptiness *(xu)* is one of the ideals in Daoism.

Heart-mind *(xin)*. The original meaning of *xin* is "heart." The heart is the place that accommodates the spirit *(shen)*. The condition of the heart affects the spirit, and vice versa. Thus *xin* also means mind, and one translates *xin* as heart-mind. It is also used in this form in Tai Chi Chuan.

Heaven and earth *(tiandi)*. Heaven is the creative power; it is round and assigned to yang. Earth is the receiving power; it is square and assigned to yin. The term "heaven and earth" *(tiandi)* usually signifies the cosmos as a whole. Together with man, heaven and earth *(tiandi)* form the Three Powers. In Chinese philosophy, as in Tai Chi Chuan, humans are required to live in harmony with heaven and earth *(tiandi)*.

Humanity *(ren)*. The word *ren* cannot be translated directly. Its character consists of two parts, "human" and "two," and therefore refers directly to interhuman relations. In literature it is translated as "humanity," "human-heartedness," "virtue," "morality," and so on. But none of the translations capture the full extent of *ren*. By humanity *(ren)* one must understand the sum of interhuman virtues, which are demanded by Confucianism. Among these virtues are filial piety, loyalty, uprightness, altruism, sincerity, and modesty. Humanity *(ren)* is part of the nature of man, but must be developed through education and guidance. In the classical Tai Chi Chuan literature one finds practically no use of the term humanity *(ren)*.

Inner nature *(xing)*. The term "inner nature" *(xing)* of man is discussed intensively in Confucianism. In the *Confucius* (or *Analects*) it is written, "Being close to each other by our inner nature *(xing)*, we separate from each other by our habits." Of the good or bad of the nature of man nothing is said. Mencius follows the idea that originally all humans are alike in their nature. From the natural behavior of humans (such as the love of children for their parents), he concludes that human nature is good. He regards the later differences between humans as the result of bad education. In contrast, Xunzi assumes that human nature is bad and can only become good through education. During the same period, other philosophers, like Gaozi, explain that humans are neither good nor bad, but that one or the other side develops according to the circumstances of life. In the Daoism of Laozi and Zhuangzi, the concept of *xing* is avoided. An individual's human nature would separate that person too much from the way *(dao)*. Instead, one refers here to the inner power *(de)*, which can be present in a person but is always connected to the whole and so refers to the way *(dao)*. In Tai Chi Chuan one tries to maintain the different aspects of one's inner nature *(xing)* by the exercises.

Inner power *(de)*. The original meaning of the term *de* is "power" or "ability." In Confucianism this became a moral power, which is translated often as "virtue." *De* marks here the Confucianist gentleman and is expressed in the five constant virtues: humanity *(ren)*, righteousness, propriety, wisdom, and faithfulness. In contrast to this, in the *Laozi, de* is a power that proceeds from the way *(dao)*. Thus it is not a specific moral quality of the individual, but is a kind of higher power. It operates by the principle of non-action *(wuwei)*. In Tai Chi Chuan the term *de* is seldom used. However, with the *jin*-power there is also a concept of an inner power.

Intention *(yi)*. Everything one holds in one's mind. In the *Zhuangzi* it is stated: "That which one can discuss is the rough aspect of the things. That which one can have in one's mind *(yi)* is the fine aspect of the things." So, sometimes it is just translated as "mind." In addition, *yi* can be understood as "imagination" or, more concretely, as "intention." In this form it is found in the *Great Learning (Daxue)*. In Tai Chi Chuan one finds all meanings.

jing. See Essence.

The martial *(wu)*. The character *wu* means "military," "martial," "violent," and "fierce." One should note that *wu* can denote both man-to-man combat and a battle of many against many, and so it has the association of war. The martial *(wu)* stands in opposition to the cultural *(wen)*.

Naturalness *(ziran)*. Literally, self so, from the two characters for "self" and "so." In the earlier Daoist tradition the search for naturalness *(ziran)* meant the retreat into nature. Beginning in the second century AD the concept changed, and one began to look for naturalness *(ziran)* in all expressions and actions of life. In Tai Chi Chuan it is also said that body and heart-mind *(xin)* are natural *(ziran)*.

Non-acting *(wuwei)*. Non-acting *(wuwei)* means not to interfere with or act against naturalness *(ziran)*. Thus one's actions conform to the principles of the cosmos. This concept is found in Daoism, but also in Confucianism. With its defensive strategy, Tai Chi Chuan follows this thought fully.

Nourishing one's life *(yangsheng)*. The goal is to attain a healthy body and mind by special exercises and to reach an ideal interaction between these two. A person who achieves this will to a large extent be unimpressed physically and mentally by his environment, and will have built the foundations for a long life. Originally not restricted to a particular school of philosophy, the term was later taken over by Daoism. The term "nourishing one's life" *(yangsheng)* is rarely found in the classical Tai Chi Chuan literature. The concept of achieving a long life by exercises for body and mind is, however, one of the main topics in Tai Chi Chuan.

Qi. In Chinese philosophy one finds very different interpretations of the term *qi*. In the *Book of Changes (Yijing)* and in the *Laozi* it is a fine substance that represents the origin of the cosmos and which is differentiated as the cosmos develops. In contrast, in the Confucianist *Xunzi* it is an undifferentiated truth, which precedes all things. In Tai Chi Chuan one can understand *qi* as breath or vitality, which is maintained by the exercises.

ren. See Humanity.

shen. See Spirit.

shi. See Full.

Sincerity *(cheng).* The term *cheng* is discussed intensively in the Confucianist *Book of the Mean (Zhongyong).* It can be translated as "sincerely" and as "authentically" or "genuinely." Sincerity *(cheng)* refers at the same time to all things and to man. In Confucianism it is stressed that it is an everlasting task for man to attain and receive sincerity *(cheng).* The Tai Chi Chuan masters also demand this from their students.

Sishu. See *Four Books.*

Spirit *(shen)*. The term *shen* has many meanings—"god," "gods," "spirit," and "soul." Depending upon the philosopher and the context, *shen* is translated differently. In Tai Chi Chuan *shen* usually means "spirit."

Taiji. The supreme ultimate. The Neo-Confucian philosopher Zhou Dunyi states: "*Wuji* (without ultimate) and then *taiji*. In movement, *taiji* creates yang. When the movement has reached its limit there is stillness. When still, *taiji* creates yin. When stillness has reached its limits, there is a return to movement. Movement and stillness alternate. Each is the root of the other." From this idea, Tai Chi Chuan *(Taijiquan)* received its name.

Ten thousand things *(wanwu)*. Ten thousand is the highest number in normal Chinese linguistic usage; therefore, the ten thousand things *(wanwu)* are the whole of everything. By things, both dead and animate are understood. Humans thus belong to the ten thousand things *(wanwu)*. In appropriate contexts, humans may also be placed in opposition to *wanwu*.

tiandi. See Heaven and earth.

wanwu. See Ten thousand things.

Way *(dao)*. Literally, "way" or "path." In addition, *dao* is translated as the "absolute," "law," "nature," or "right way" of man. In Daoism the way *(dao)* is understood as a principle from which the cosmos rises. Generally in Confucianism "the way of heaven" *(tian zhi dao)* becomes more "the right way of man" *(ren zhi dao)*. Thus Confucius describes *dao* as also the way of a certain person. He speaks of the way *(dao)* of the kings Wen and Wu. Therefore, the way *(dao)* assumes a moral quality that a Confucianist gentleman must attain. If one does not achieve this quality, one diverges from the way *(dao)*. In Tai Chi Chuan the way *(dao)* is a combination of the Daoist and the Confucian concepts.

wen. See The cultural.

Wujing. See *Five Classics.*

wu. See The martial.

wuwei. See Non-acting.

wuxing. See Five phases.

xin. See Heart-mind.

xing. See Inner nature.

xu. See Full and empty.

yangsheng. See Nourishing one's life.

yi. See Intention.

Yin and yang. The character for yin contains the representation of a hill in the shade and so designates the shady. The character for yang consists of diagonal sunbeams on a hill and thus stands for the sunny. From this are derived yin and yang as the polar forces inherent in the cosmos. Yang becomes the light, the heaven, the creative, and the male, and yin the dark, the earth, the receiving, and the female. The use of yin and yang as philosophical terms began in the fourth century BC. They are found in the *Great Appendix* of the *Book of Changes (Yijing)* and in the *Zhuangzi,* but are also used more widely in calendars and in the *Book of Odes (Shijing).* The name Tai Chi Chuan *(Taijiquan)* means that this martial art is based on the principle of *taiji.* Yin and yang are created by *taiji* and are therefore of the greatest importance for Tai Chi Chuan.

ziran. See Naturalness.

About North Atlantic Books

North Atlantic Books (NAB) is an independent, nonprofit publisher committed to a bold exploration of the relationships between mind, body, spirit, and nature. Founded in 1974, NAB aims to nurture a holistic view of the arts, sciences, humanities, and healing. To make a donation or to learn more about our books, authors, events, and newsletter, please visit www.northatlanticbooks.com.

North Atlantic Books is the publishing arm of the Society for the Study of Native Arts and Sciences, a 501(c)(3) nonprofit educational organization that promotes cross-cultural perspectives linking scientific, social, and artistic fields. To learn how you can support us, please visit our website.